PRESSURE CANNI

MEALS MADE EASY

TABLE OF CONTENTS

Understanding Pressure Canning..5

    Equipment Needed for Pressure Canning: 6

    Safety Precautions and Best Practices 8

Essential Tools and Ingredients..11

Step-by-Step Canning Process 14

Advanced Techniques and Tips 17

PRESSURE CANNING RECIPES...19

    1. Classic Tomato Sauce..19

    2. Spicy Pickled Green Beans 20

    3. Chicken Vegetable Soup...21

    4. Peach Jam..22

    5. Beef Stew...22

    6. Apple Pie Filling 24

    7. Cranberry Orange Sauce 25

    8. Chili Con Carne 26

    9. Ratatouille...27

    10. Lemon Curd 28

    11. Butternut Squash Soup...29

    12. Sweet Corn Relish 30

    13. Pineapple Salsa 31

    14. Apple Butter..32

15. Cranberry Sauce 33

16. Pear Vanilla Jam 34

17. Ratatouille Sauce 35

19. Carrot Cake Jam 37

20. Garlic Dill Pickles 38

21. Chunky Applesauce...39

22. Ginger Pear Chutney 40

23. Tomato Basil Soup...41

24. Mango Salsa 42

25. Peach BBQ Sauce 43

26. Mixed Berry Jam 44

27. Vegetable Stock..45

28. Pickled Beets 46

29. Peach Salsa 47

30. Lemon Garlic Asparagus 48

31. Mango Chutney 49

32. Cinnamon Applesauce 50

33. Tomato Jam 51

34. Pumpkin Butter 52

35. Ginger Pear Preserves...54

36. Spicy Pickled Okra 55

37. Honey Cinnamon Pear Butter 56

38. Peach Pie Filling 57

39. Chunky Tomato Sauce 58

40. Orange Marmalade 59

41. Black Bean and Corn Salsa 60

42. Strawberry Rhubarb Jam 61

43. Roasted Red Pepper Sauce 62

44. Peach Chutney 63

45. Spiced Pear Butter 64

46. Cranberry Orange Relish 65

47. Mango Habanero Salsa 66

48. Apple Pie Filling 67

49. Spicy Tomato Jam 68

50. Pineapple Jalapeno Jelly 69

UNDERSTANDING PRESSURE CANNING

Pressure canning is a time-tested method for preserving foods that requires a specialized piece of equipment known as a pressure canner. Unlike traditional boiling water canning, which is suitable for high-acid foods like fruits and pickles, pressure canning is necessary for low-acid foods such as vegetables, meats, poultry, and soups. Understanding the principles and mechanics of pressure canning is essential for ensuring the safety and success of your preserved foods. Pressure canning has a rich history dating back to the early 19th century when French chef Nicolas Appert developed a method of preserving food in sealed glass jars. However, it wasn't until the invention of the pressure canner by French inventor Denis Papin in 1679 that the modern concept of pressure canning began to take shape. Over the years, advancements in technology and food safety regulations have refined the process, making it accessible to home cooks around the world. At its core, pressure canning relies on the principle of heat transfer to destroy harmful microorganisms and enzymes that cause food spoilage. By placing sealed jars of food in a pressure canner filled with water and subjecting them to high temperatures and pressure, the contents of the jars are effectively sterilized, ensuring their long-term preservation. The combination of heat and pressure raises the boiling point of water, allowing for the safe processing of low-acid foods at temperatures above 240°F (116°C).

Equipment Needed for Pressure Canning:

Unlike boiling water canning, which can be done with basic kitchen equipment, pressure canning requires specialized tools to ensure safety and effectiveness. Key equipment includes:

- Pressure canner: A large, heavy-duty pot with a locking lid and pressure gauge or dial.
- Mason jars: Glass jars specifically designed for canning, available in various sizes.
- Jar rack: A metal rack that holds jars in place inside the pressure canner, preventing them from touching the bottom.
- Canning utensils: Tools such as jar lifters, funnels, and bubble removers for filling and handling jars safely.

- Pressure gauge: An essential component of the pressure canner for monitoring and regulating pressure during processing.

Importance of Proper Sanitation:

Maintaining strict sanitation practices is crucial when pressure canning to prevent the growth of harmful bacteria and ensure the safety of preserved foods. Before starting the canning process, it's essential to thoroughly clean and sterilize all equipment, including jars, lids, and utensils. Additionally, washing and preparing fresh ingredients with clean hands and surfaces helps minimize the risk of contamination.

Key Concepts and Terminology:

To navigate the world of pressure canning effectively, it's helpful to familiarize yourself with key concepts and terminology, including:

- Altitude adjustments: Because water boils at lower temperatures at higher altitudes, adjustments to processing times or pressures may be necessary to achieve safe canning results.
- Headspace: The empty space between the top of the food and the rim of the jar, which allows for expansion during processing and proper sealing.
- Processing time: The duration that jars must remain in the pressure canner at the specified pressure to achieve proper sterilization.
- Venting: Releasing steam from the pressure canner before sealing to eliminate air pockets and establish a proper pressure environment.

Safety Precautions and Best Practices

Safety is paramount when it comes to pressure canning. Understanding and adhering to proper safety precautions and best practices is essential to ensure the preservation of food and protect against potential health risks. This chapter provides an in-depth overview of safety measures and guidelines to follow throughout the pressure canning process. Pressure canning involves exposing food to high temperatures and pressures to achieve proper sterilization. Failure to adhere to safety guidelines can result in underprocessed foods, which may harbor harmful bacteria such as Clostridium botulinum, leading to foodborne illness. Additionally, improper sealing or processing techniques can result in spoilage and loss of food. Before using a pressure canner, familiarize yourself with its specific features and instructions.

Some key safety considerations include:

- Checking for damage: Inspect the pressure canner for any signs of damage or wear before each use, including cracks, dents, or rust.
- Following manufacturer's instructions: Always refer to the manufacturer's guidelines for proper operation, including assembly, filling instructions, and maintenance.
- Monitoring pressure: Keep a close eye on the pressure gauge or dial throughout the canning process to ensure it remains within the recommended range.
- Releasing pressure safely: After processing is complete, allow the pressure canner to cool naturally before attempting to release pressure or remove the lid.

Ensuring Proper Sealing:

Proper sealing is crucial for maintaining the integrity and safety of canned foods. Follow these tips to ensure a secure seal:

- Using new lids: Always use new, unused lids for each canning session to ensure a reliable seal. Used lids may not form a proper seal, increasing the risk of spoilage.
- Checking for defects: Inspect lids for any signs of defects, such as dents or warping, which may prevent a proper seal.
- Applying bands correctly: Finger-tighten bands onto jars before processing, ensuring they are snug but not overly tight. Overtightening can prevent air from escaping, hindering proper sealing.

Preventing Spoilage and Contamination:

- Proper sanitation and handling techniques are essential for preventing spoilage and contamination throughout the canning process. Some best practices include:
- Washing hands and surfaces: Thoroughly wash hands and surfaces with hot, soapy water before handling ingredients or equipment to prevent cross-contamination.
- Using fresh ingredients: Start with fresh, high-quality ingredients free from mold, rot, or bruising to ensure the best results.
- Avoiding cross-contamination: Keep raw and cooked foods separate during preparation and processing to prevent the spread of bacteria.

Once jars have been properly processed and sealed, it's important to store them correctly to maintain their quality and safety.

Consider the following guidelines:

- Labeling and dating jars: Clearly label each jar with its contents and the date of processing to track freshness and rotation.
- Storing in a cool, dark place: Store canned goods in a cool, dry pantry away from direct sunlight and heat sources to prolong shelf life.
- Checking for signs of spoilage: Before consuming canned goods, inspect jars for any signs of spoilage, including bulging lids, off-odors, or visible mold.

ESSENTIAL TOOLS AND INGREDIENTS

To embark on your pressure canning journey successfully, it's crucial to have the right tools and quality ingredients at your disposal. In this chapter, we'll explore the essential equipment needed for pressure canning and discuss the wide array of ingredients suitable for preserving in jars.

1. Pressure Canner: The pressure canner is the cornerstone of the pressure canning process. It's a large, heavy-duty pot with a locking lid and a pressure gauge or dial. When choosing a pressure canner, opt for one that's specifically designed for canning and meets safety standards. Look for features such as sturdy construction, easy-to-read pressure gauge, and a reliable sealing mechanism.

2. Mason Jars: Mason jars are the preferred vessel for pressure canning due to their durability and ability to withstand high temperatures. Available in various sizes, from half-pint to quart-sized jars, they're perfect for preserving a wide range of foods, from fruits and vegetables to soups and sauces. Choose jars that are free from chips, cracks, or defects, and always use new lids for each canning session to ensure a proper seal.

3. Jar Rack: A jar rack is an indispensable accessory for pressure canning as it helps to keep jars upright and stable during processing. Look for a rack that's designed to fit inside your pressure canner and holds jars securely in place, preventing them from touching each other or the bottom of the canner. This ensures even heat distribution and reduces the risk of jar breakage.

4. Canning Utensils: Several canning utensils are essential for safe and efficient pressure canning:

- Jar lifter: A pair of tongs with a rubberized grip designed to lift hot jars in and out of the canner safely.

- Canning funnel: A wide-mouthed funnel that helps to fill jars cleanly and efficiently, minimizing spills and mess.

- Bubble remover: A long, slender tool used to release air bubbles trapped inside jars before sealing.

- Magnetic lid lifter: A handy tool for safely lifting hot lids out of simmering water and placing them onto jars without touching them.

5 Ingredients for Pressure Canning:

When it comes to pressure canning, the possibilities are endless. Virtually any type of food can be preserved in jars using this method, from fresh produce to cooked meals. Some popular ingredients for pressure canning include:

- Fruits: Apples, pears, peaches, berries, and citrus fruits can be canned as whole fruits, jams, jellies, or fruit spreads.

- Vegetables: Tomatoes, green beans, carrots, corn, and peppers are commonly canned either as individual vegetables or in mixed combinations.

- Soups and stews: Homemade soups, stews, and chili can be prepared in large batches and canned for quick and convenient meals.

- Meats and poultry: Cooked meats such as chicken, beef, pork, and seafood can be canned for long-term storage, ideal for adding protein to meals.

6. Sourcing Quality Ingredients: When selecting ingredients for pressure canning, prioritize freshness and quality. Choose ripe, blemish-free fruits and vegetables at their peak of flavor and nutritional value. If possible, opt for organic or locally sourced produce to support sustainable farming practices and minimize exposure to pesticides and chemicals.

STEP-BY-STEP CANNING PROCESS

This chapter covers the step-by-step process of pressure canning, from preparing your ingredients to sealing jars for long-term storage. By following these clear and concise instructions, you'll be well-equipped to safely and efficiently preserve a variety of foods using the pressure canning method.

1. Prepare Your Ingredients: Before you begin pressure canning, it's essential to prepare your ingredients thoroughly. This may include washing, peeling, slicing, and blanching fruits and vegetables, as well as cooking meats and soups to the desired consistency. Ensure that all ingredients are fresh, high-quality, and free from any signs of spoilage or damage.

2. Sterilize Your Equipment: Proper sanitation is critical when pressure canning to prevent the growth of harmful bacteria and ensure the safety of your preserved foods. Before starting the canning process, wash all jars, lids, and utensils in hot, soapy water, then rinse them thoroughly. Alternatively, you can sterilize your equipment by boiling it in water for 10 minutes or running it through a dishwasher cycle.

3. Fill Jars with Ingredients: Once your ingredients are prepared, it's time to fill your jars. Using a canning funnel, carefully ladle the prepared ingredients into clean, sterilized jars, leaving the recommended headspace at the top. Headspace requirements vary depending on the type of food being canned, so be sure to refer to your recipe or canning guidelines for specific instructions.

4. Remove Air Bubbles and Adjust Headspace: After filling the jars, use a bubble remover or a non-metallic utensil to release any trapped air bubbles by running it along the inside edge of the jar. Then, use a clean, damp cloth to wipe the rims of the jars to remove any food residue or spills. Finally, use a headspace tool or ruler to ensure that the headspace is correct, adding or removing food as needed.

5. Apply Lids and Bands: Once the jars are filled and the headspace is adjusted, it's time to apply the lids and bands. Place a new, unused lid on top of each jar, ensuring that the sealing compound is in contact with the rim of the jar. Then, screw the bands onto the jars until they are fingertip tight — tight enough to hold the lid in place, but not too tight to prevent air from escaping during processing.

6. Process Jars in the Pressure Canner: With your jars filled, sealed, and ready to go, it's time to process them in the pressure canner. Follow these steps:

1. Place the filled jars on the jar rack inside the pressure canner, ensuring they are spaced apart and not touching each other or the sides of the canner.
2. Add the specified amount of water to the pressure canner, as outlined in your canner's instructions.
3. Lock the lid in place and bring the pressure canner to the specified pressure according to your recipe or altitude guidelines.
4. Once the canner reaches the desired pressure, begin timing the processing according to your recipe or canning guidelines.
5. After the processing time is complete, turn off the heat and allow the pressure canner to depressurize naturally before removing the lid.

7. Cool and Store Jars: After depressurizing, carefully remove the jars from the pressure canner using a jar lifter and place them on a clean towel or cooling rack to cool completely. As the jars cool, you may hear the satisfying "ping" of the lids sealing—a sign that your jars have been properly processed. Once cooled, check the seals by pressing down on the center of each lid. If the lid is firm and does not flex, the jar is sealed and ready for storage. Any unsealed jars should be refrigerated and consumed within a few days.

ADVANCED TECHNIQUES AND TIPS

1. Flavor Infusion Methods: Elevate your canned creations by experimenting with flavor infusion methods. Consider adding herbs, spices, citrus zest, or aromatics like garlic and ginger to your jars before filling them with ingredients. As the jars process in the pressure canner, these flavor-enhancing elements will infuse the contents, resulting in more complex and delicious flavors.

2. Using Alternative Ingredients and Substitutions: Don't be afraid to get creative with your pressure canning recipes by using alternative ingredients and substitutions. For example, you can swap out traditional grains like rice or pasta for quinoa or barley in soups and stews. Similarly, consider using alternative sweeteners like honey or maple syrup in fruit preserves or jams for a unique twist.

3. Adapting Recipes for Dietary Restrictions: Pressure canning is versatile enough to accommodate a wide range of dietary restrictions and preferences. Whether you're following a gluten-free, dairy-free, or vegan diet, there are plenty of options for pressure-canned jar meals. Look for recipes that use naturally gluten-free grains and starches, incorporate dairy-free alternatives, or focus on plant-based proteins and vegetables.

4. Creative Presentation Ideas: Transform your pressure-canned jar meals into visually stunning and giftable creations with creative presentation ideas. Consider layering colorful ingredients in clear glass jars to showcase their vibrant hues, or embellishing jar lids with decorative labels or fabric covers for a personalized touch. You can also arrange jars in gift baskets or boxes and accompany them with recipe cards or serving suggestions for a thoughtful and practical gift.

5. Exploring International Flavors: Expand your culinary horizons by exploring international flavors and cuisines in your pressure canning recipes. Experiment

with spices, seasonings, and ingredients from around the world to create unique and flavorful jar meals inspired by global cuisines. Whether you're craving the bold flavors of Indian curry, the aromatic spices of Moroccan tagine, or the comforting warmth of Italian minestrone, the possibilities are endless.

6. Scaling Up and Batch Cooking: Maximize the efficiency of your pressure canning endeavors by scaling up recipes and batch cooking. Investing a little extra time and effort upfront to prepare large batches of soups, stews, or sauces allows you to fill multiple jars at once, saving time and energy in the long run. Plus, having a stash of pressure-canned jar meals on hand makes meal planning and weeknight dinners a breeze.

7. Gifting Pressure-Canned Jar Meals: Share the joy of homemade meals with friends and family by gifting pressure-canned jar meals for special occasions or holidays. Whether it's a jar of hearty soup for a sick friend, a batch of homemade jam for a hostess gift, or a collection of themed jar meals for a housewarming present, homemade canned goods are always appreciated and well-received.

PRESSURE CANNING RECIPES

1. Classic Tomato Sauce

Ingredients:

- 10 lbs ripe tomatoes, washed and chopped
- 2 onions, finely chopped
- 4 cloves garlic, minced
- 1/4 cup olive oil
- 2 tsp salt
- 1 tsp black pepper
- 2 tbsp fresh basil, chopped

Instructions:

1. Heat olive oil in a large pot over medium heat. Add onions and garlic, sauté until soft.
2. Add chopped tomatoes, salt, and pepper. Cook until tomatoes break down, about 30 minutes.
3. Stir in fresh basil and cook for an additional 5 minutes.
4. Ladle hot sauce into sterilized jars, leaving 1/2-inch headspace.
5. Wipe jar rims, apply lids, and tighten bands finger-tight.
6. Process jars in a pressure canner at 10 pounds pressure for 35 minutes for pint jars or 40 minutes for quart jars.
7. Allow jars to cool, then check seals and store in a cool, dark place.

Shelf Life: Up to 1 year.

2. Spicy Pickled Green Beans

Ingredients:

- 2 lbs green beans, trimmed
- 2 cups white vinegar
- 2 cups water
- 4 cloves garlic, sliced
- 2 tbsp pickling salt
- 2 tsp dill seeds
- 2 tsp red pepper flakes

Instructions:

1. In a saucepan, combine vinegar, water, garlic, pickling salt, dill seeds, and red pepper flakes. Bring to a boil.
2. Pack green beans into sterilized jars, standing them upright.
3. Pour hot pickling liquid over beans, leaving 1/2-inch headspace.
4. Wipe jar rims, apply lids, and tighten bands finger-tight.
5. Process jars in a pressure canner at 10 pounds pressure for 10 minutes for pint jars or 15 minutes for quart jars.
6. Allow jars to cool, then check seals and store in a cool, dark place.

Shelf Life: Up to 1 year.

3. Chicken Vegetable Soup

Ingredients:

- 2 lbs boneless, skinless chicken breasts, cubed
- 6 cups chicken broth
- 2 cups carrots, diced
- 2 cups celery, diced
- 2 cups potatoes, diced
- 1 cup onion, chopped
- 2 cloves garlic, minced
- 2 tsp salt
- 1 tsp black pepper
- 2 bay leaves

Instructions:

1. In a large pot, combine chicken, chicken broth, carrots, celery, potatoes, onion, garlic, salt, pepper, and bay leaves. Bring to a boil.
2. Reduce heat and simmer for 20 minutes.
3. Ladle hot soup into sterilized jars, leaving 1-inch headspace.
4. Wipe jar rims, apply lids, and tighten bands finger-tight.
5. Process jars in a pressure canner at 10 pounds pressure for 75 minutes for pint jars or 90 minutes for quart jars.
6. Allow jars to cool, then check seals and store in a cool, dark place.

Shelf Life: Up to 1 year.

4. Peach Jam

Ingredients:

- 4 lbs peaches, peeled, pitted, and chopped
- 4 cups granulated sugar
- 1/4 cup lemon juice
- 1 tsp vanilla extract (optional)

Instructions:

1. In a large pot, combine chopped peaches, sugar, lemon juice, and vanilla extract. Let sit for 2 hours to allow the sugar to draw out the juices.
2. Bring peach mixture to a boil over medium-high heat, stirring frequently.
3. Continue boiling until jam reaches gel stage, about 20-30 minutes.
4. Ladle hot jam into sterilized jars, leaving 1/4-inch headspace.
5. Wipe jar rims, apply lids, and tighten bands finger-tight.
6. Process jars in a pressure canner at 5 pounds pressure for 5 minutes.
7. Allow jars to cool, then check seals and store in a cool, dark place.

Shelf Life: Up to 1 year.

5. Beef Stew

Ingredients:

- 3 lbs beef stew meat, cubed

- 4 cups beef broth
- 2 cups carrots, sliced
- 2 cups potatoes, diced
- 1 cup celery, chopped
- 1 cup onion, chopped
- 2 cloves garlic, minced
- 2 tsp salt
- 1 tsp black pepper
- 2 bay leaves

Instructions:

1. In a large pot, combine beef stew meat, beef broth, carrots, potatoes, celery, onion, garlic, salt, pepper, and bay leaves. Bring to a boil.
2. Reduce heat and simmer for 20 minutes.
3. Ladle hot stew into sterilized jars, leaving 1-inch headspace.
4. Wipe jar rims, apply lids, and tighten bands finger-tight.
5. Process jars in a pressure canner at 10 pounds pressure for 90 minutes for pint jars or 105 minutes for quart jars.
6. Allow jars to cool, then check seals and store in a cool, dark place.

Shelf Life: Up to 1 year.

6. Apple Pie Filling

Ingredients:

- 10 cups sliced peeled apples
- 2 cups granulated sugar
- 1/2 cup all-purpose flour
- 1 tsp ground cinnamon
- 1/4 tsp ground nutmeg
- 1/4 tsp salt
- 4 cups water
- 1/2 cup lemon juice

Instructions:

1. In a large bowl, combine sliced apples, sugar, flour, cinnamon, nutmeg, and salt. Toss to coat apples evenly.
2. In a saucepan, bring water and lemon juice to a boil.
3. Add apple mixture to boiling water and cook for 5 minutes, stirring occasionally.
4. Ladle hot apple pie filling into sterilized jars, leaving 1-inch headspace.
5. Wipe jar rims, apply lids, and tighten bands finger-tight.
6. Process jars in a pressure canner at 10 pounds pressure for 25 minutes for pint jars or 30 minutes for quart jars.
7. Allow jars to cool, then check seals and store in a cool, dark place.

Shelf Life: Up to 1 year.

7. Cranberry Orange Sauce

Ingredients:

- 4 cups fresh or frozen cranberries
- 2 cups granulated sugar
- 1 cup orange juice
- Zest of 1 orange
- 1/2 tsp ground cinnamon
- 1/4 tsp ground cloves

Instructions:

1. In a saucepan, combine cranberries, sugar, orange juice, orange zest, cinnamon, and cloves. Bring to a boil over medium heat.
2. Reduce heat and simmer for 10-15 minutes, stirring occasionally, until cranberries burst and sauce thickens.
3. Ladle hot cranberry orange sauce into sterilized jars, leaving 1/4-inch headspace.
4. Wipe jar rims, apply lids, and tighten bands finger-tight.
5. Process jars in a pressure canner at 10 pounds pressure for 10 minutes.
6. Allow jars to cool, then check seals and store in a cool, dark place.

Shelf Life: Up to 1 year.

8. Chili Con Carne

Ingredients:

- 3 lbs ground beef
- 2 onions, chopped
- 4 cloves garlic, minced
- 2 cups kidney beans, cooked
- 2 cups black beans, cooked
- 4 cups tomato sauce
- 2 cups beef broth
- 1/4 cup chili powder
- 2 tsp ground cumin
- 2 tsp paprika
- 2 tsp salt
- 1 tsp black pepper

Instructions:

1. In a large pot, brown ground beef over medium heat. Add onions and garlic, sauté until soft.
2. Stir in cooked kidney beans, black beans, tomato sauce, beef broth, chili powder, cumin, paprika, salt, and black pepper.
3. Bring chili to a simmer and cook for 10 minutes, stirring occasionally.
4. Ladle hot chili into sterilized jars, leaving 1-inch headspace.
5. Wipe jar rims, apply lids, and tighten bands finger-tight.

6. Process jars in a pressure canner at 10 pounds pressure for 90 minutes for pint jars or 105 minutes for quart jars.

7. Allow jars to cool, then check seals and store in a cool, dark place.

Shelf Life: Up to 1 year.

9. Ratatouille

Ingredients:

- 4 cups eggplant, diced
- 4 cups zucchini, diced
- 2 cups bell peppers, diced
- 2 cups tomatoes, diced
- 1 cup onions, diced
- 4 cloves garlic, minced
- 1/4 cup olive oil
- 2 tsp dried basil
- 2 tsp dried oregano
- 2 tsp salt
- 1 tsp black pepper

Instructions:

1. In a large pot, heat olive oil over medium heat. Add onions and garlic, sauté until soft.

2. Add diced eggplant, zucchini, bell peppers, and tomatoes to the pot. Stir in basil, oregano, salt, and black pepper.

3. Cook ratatouille over medium heat for 20-25 minutes, stirring occasionally, until vegetables are tender.

4. Ladle hot ratatouille into sterilized jars, leaving 1-inch headspace.

5. Wipe jar rims, apply lids, and tighten bands finger-tight.

6. Process jars in a pressure canner at 10 pounds pressure for 40 minutes for pint jars or 45 minutes for quart jars.

7. Allow jars to cool, then check seals and store in a cool, dark place.

Shelf Life: Up to 1 year.

10. Lemon Curd

Ingredients:

- Zest of 4 lemons
- 1 cup freshly squeezed lemon juice
- 1 1/2 cups granulated sugar
- 6 large eggs
- 3/4 cup unsalted butter, cubed

Instructions:

1. In a heatproof bowl, whisk together lemon zest, lemon juice, sugar, and eggs.

2. Place bowl over a pot of simmering water (double boiler) and cook, stirring constantly, until mixture thickens and coats the back of a spoon, about 10-15 minutes.

3. Remove bowl from heat and stir in cubed butter until melted and incorporated.

4. Ladle hot lemon curd into sterilized jars, leaving 1/4-inch headspace.

5. Wipe jar rims, apply lids, and tighten bands finger-tight.

6. Process jars in a pressure canner at 5 pounds pressure for 10 minutes.

7. Allow jars to cool, then check seals and store in a cool, dark place.

Shelf Life: Up to 6 months.

11. Butternut Squash Soup

Ingredients:

- 4 lbs butternut squash, peeled, seeded, and diced
- 2 cups carrots, diced
- 2 cups onions, chopped
- 4 cloves garlic, minced
- 6 cups vegetable broth
- 1 tsp ground ginger
- 1/2 tsp ground nutmeg
- Salt and pepper to taste

Instructions:

- In a large pot, combine butternut squash, carrots, onions, garlic, vegetable broth, ginger, nutmeg, salt, and pepper.
- Bring to a boil, then reduce heat and simmer for 20-25 minutes, until vegetables are tender.
- Use an immersion blender to puree the soup until smooth.
- Ladle hot soup into sterilized jars, leaving 1-inch headspace.
- Wipe jar rims, apply lids, and tighten bands finger-tight.
- Process jars in a pressure canner at 10 pounds pressure for 75 minutes for pint jars or 90 minutes for quart jars.
- Allow jars to cool, then check seals and store in a cool, dark place.

Shelf Life: Up to 1 year.

12. Sweet Corn Relish

Ingredients:

- 8 cups sweet corn kernels (fresh or frozen)
- 2 cups bell peppers, diced (assorted colors)
- 2 cups onions, diced
- 2 cups celery, diced
- 2 cups apple cider vinegar
- 1 1/2 cups granulated sugar
- 1/4 cup mustard seeds

- 2 tbsp celery seeds
- 1 tbsp turmeric
- 2 tsp salt

Instructions:

1. In a large pot, combine sweet corn kernels, bell peppers, onions, celery, apple cider vinegar, sugar, mustard seeds, celery seeds, turmeric, and salt.
2. Bring mixture to a boil over medium-high heat, then reduce heat and simmer for 10-15 minutes, stirring occasionally.
3. Ladle hot relish into sterilized jars, leaving 1/2-inch headspace.
4. Wipe jar rims, apply lids, and tighten bands finger-tight.
5. Process jars in a pressure canner at 10 pounds pressure for 15 minutes.
6. Allow jars to cool, then check seals and store in a cool, dark place.

Shelf Life: Up to 1 year.

13. Pineapple Salsa

Ingredients:

- 4 cups diced pineapple
- 2 cups bell peppers, diced (assorted colors)
- 1 cup red onion, diced
- 1 cup cilantro, chopped
- 1/2 cup jalapeno peppers, seeded and diced

- 1/4 cup lime juice
- 1 tsp salt

Instructions:

1. In a large bowl, combine diced pineapple, bell peppers, red onion, cilantro, jalapeno peppers, lime juice, and salt. Mix well.
2. Ladle salsa into sterilized jars, leaving 1/2-inch headspace.
3. Wipe jar rims, apply lids, and tighten bands finger-tight.
4. Process jars in a pressure canner at 5 pounds pressure for 10 minutes.
5. Allow jars to cool, then check seals and store in a cool, dark place.

Shelf Life: Up to 1 year.

14. Apple Butter

Ingredients:

- 5 lbs apples, peeled, cored, and sliced
- 2 cups apple cider
- 2 cups granulated sugar
- 1 tbsp ground cinnamon
- 1/2 tsp ground cloves
- 1/2 tsp ground nutmeg

Instructions:

1. In a large pot, combine sliced apples and apple cider. Bring to a boil, then reduce heat and simmer for 20-30 minutes, until apples are soft.

2. Use an immersion blender to puree the cooked apples until smooth.

3. Add sugar, cinnamon, cloves, and nutmeg to the pot, stirring to combine.

4. Continue cooking over medium heat, stirring frequently, until apple butter thickens to desired consistency, about 1-2 hours.

5. Ladle hot apple butter into sterilized jars, leaving 1/4-inch headspace.

6. Wipe jar rims, apply lids, and tighten bands finger-tight.

7. Process jars in a pressure canner at 5 pounds pressure for 10 minutes.

8. Allow jars to cool, then check seals and store in a cool, dark place.

Shelf Life: Up to 1 year.

15. Cranberry Sauce

Ingredients:

- 4 cups fresh or frozen cranberries
- 2 cups granulated sugar
- 1 cup orange juice
- Zest of 1 orange
- 1/2 tsp ground cinnamon
- 1/4 tsp ground cloves

Instructions:

1. In a saucepan, combine cranberries, sugar, orange juice, orange zest, cinnamon, and cloves. Bring to a boil over medium heat.

2. Reduce heat and simmer for 10-15 minutes, stirring occasionally, until cranberries burst and sauce thickens.

3. Ladle hot cranberry sauce into sterilized jars, leaving 1/4-inch headspace.

4. Wipe jar rims, apply lids, and tighten bands finger-tight.

5. Process jars in a pressure canner at 10 pounds pressure for 10 minutes.

6. Allow jars to cool, then check seals and store in a cool, dark place.

Shelf Life: Up to 1 year.

16. Pear Vanilla Jam

Ingredients:

- 4 cups ripe pears, peeled, cored, and diced
- 2 cups granulated sugar
- 1/4 cup lemon juice
- 1 vanilla bean, split and seeds scraped

Instructions:

1. In a large pot, combine diced pears, sugar, lemon juice, vanilla bean seeds, and scraped vanilla bean pod. Let sit for 2 hours to allow the sugar to draw out the juices.

2. Bring pear mixture to a boil over medium-high heat, stirring frequently.

3. Continue boiling until jam reaches gel stage, about 20-30 minutes.

4. Ladle hot jam into sterilized jars, leaving 1/4-inch headspace.

5. Wipe jar rims, apply lids, and tighten bands finger-tight.

6. Process jars in a pressure canner at 5 pounds pressure for 5 minutes.

7. Allow jars to cool, then check seals and store in a cool, dark place.

Shelf Life: Up to 1 year.

17. Ratatouille Sauce

Ingredients:

- 4 cups diced eggplant
- 4 cups diced zucchini
- 2 cups diced bell peppers (assorted colors)
- 2 cups diced tomatoes
- 1 cup diced onions
- 4 cloves garlic, minced
- 1/4 cup olive oil
- 2 tsp dried basil
- 2 tsp dried oregano
- 2 tsp salt
- 1 tsp black pepper

Instructions:

1. In a large pot, heat olive oil over medium heat. Add onions and garlic, sauté until soft.

2. Add diced eggplant, zucchini, bell peppers, and tomatoes to the pot. Stir in basil, oregano, salt, and black pepper.

3. Cook ratatouille sauce over medium heat for 20-25 minutes, stirring occasionally, until vegetables are tender.

4. Ladle hot sauce into sterilized jars, leaving 1-inch headspace.

5. Wipe jar rims, apply lids, and tighten bands finger-tight.

6. Process jars in a pressure canner at 10 pounds pressure for 40 minutes for pint jars or 45 minutes for quart jars.

7. Allow jars to cool, then check seals and store in a cool, dark place.

Shelf Life: Up to 1 year.

18. Blueberry Pie Filling

Ingredients:

- 8 cups fresh or frozen blueberries
- 2 cups granulated sugar
- 1/2 cup cornstarch
- 1/4 cup lemon juice
- 1 tsp ground cinnamon
- 1/4 tsp ground nutmeg

Instructions:

1. In a large pot, combine blueberries, sugar, cornstarch, lemon juice, cinnamon, and nutmeg. Cook over medium heat until mixture thickens, stirring constantly.
2. Remove from heat and let cool slightly.
3. Ladle hot pie filling into sterilized jars, leaving 1-inch headspace.
4. Wipe jar rims, apply lids, and tighten bands finger-tight.
5. Process jars in a pressure canner at 10 pounds pressure for 20 minutes.
6. Allow jars to cool, then check seals and store in a cool, dark place.

Shelf Life: Up to 1 year.

19. Carrot Cake Jam

Ingredients:

- 4 cups shredded carrots
- 2 cups crushed pineapple, undrained
- 1 cup raisins
- 2 cups granulated sugar
- 1/4 cup lemon juice
- 1 tsp ground cinnamon
- 1/2 tsp ground nutmeg
- 1/4 tsp ground cloves

Instructions:

1. In a large pot, combine shredded carrots, crushed pineapple, raisins, sugar, lemon juice, cinnamon, nutmeg, and cloves. Bring to a boil over medium-high heat.

2. Reduce heat and simmer for 20-25 minutes, until mixture thickens, stirring occasionally.

3. Ladle hot jam into sterilized jars, leaving 1/4-inch headspace.

4. Wipe jar rims, apply lids, and tighten bands finger-tight.

5. Process jars in a pressure canner at 5 pounds pressure for 10 minutes.

6. Allow jars to cool, then check seals and store in a cool, dark place.

Shelf Life: Up to 1 year.

20. Garlic Dill Pickles

Ingredients:

- 4 lbs pickling cucumbers, washed and sliced
- 8 cloves garlic, peeled and halved
- 4 sprigs fresh dill
- 4 cups water
- 4 cups white vinegar
- 1/2 cup pickling salt
- 2 tbsp pickling spice

Instructions:

1. In each sterilized jar, place 2 garlic halves and 1 sprig of dill.
2. Pack cucumber slices into jars, leaving 1/2-inch headspace.
3. In a saucepan, combine water, vinegar, pickling salt, and pickling spice. Bring to a boil.
4. Pour hot brine over cucumbers, covering them completely and leaving 1/2-inch headspace.
5. Wipe jar rims, apply lids, and tighten bands finger-tight.
6. Process jars in a pressure canner at 10 pounds pressure for 10 minutes.
7. Allow jars to cool, then check seals and store in a cool, dark place.

Shelf Life: Up to 1 year.

21. Chunky Applesauce

Ingredients:

- 5 lbs apples, peeled, cored, and chopped
- 1 cup water
- 1/2 cup granulated sugar (optional)
- 2 tsp ground cinnamon

Instructions:

1. In a large pot, combine chopped apples and water. Cook over medium heat until apples are soft, about 20-25 minutes.
2. Use a potato masher or immersion blender to mash apples to desired consistency.
3. Stir in sugar and cinnamon, if using.
4. Ladle hot applesauce into sterilized jars, leaving 1/2-inch headspace.
5. Wipe jar rims, apply lids, and tighten bands finger-tight.
6. Process jars in a pressure canner at 5 pounds pressure for 5 minutes.
7. Allow jars to cool, then check seals and store in a cool, dark place.

Shelf Life: Up to 1 year.

22. Ginger Pear Chutney

Ingredients:

- 4 cups diced pears
- 2 cups apple cider vinegar
- 2 cups brown sugar
- 1 cup raisins
- 1 cup chopped onion
- 1/4 cup crystallized ginger, chopped
- 2 cloves garlic, minced
- 1 tsp mustard seeds

- 1 tsp ground cinnamon
- 1/2 tsp ground cloves
- 1/2 tsp salt

Instructions:

1. In a large pot, combine diced pears, apple cider vinegar, brown sugar, raisins, onion, crystallized ginger, garlic, mustard seeds, cinnamon, cloves, and salt.
2. Bring mixture to a boil over medium-high heat, then reduce heat and simmer for 45-60 minutes, stirring occasionally, until chutney thickens.
3. Ladle hot chutney into sterilized jars, leaving 1/2-inch headspace.
4. Wipe jar rims, apply lids, and tighten bands finger-tight.
5. Process jars in a pressure canner at 10 pounds pressure for 10 minutes.
6. Allow jars to cool, then check seals and store in a cool, dark place.

Shelf Life: Up to 1 year.

23. Tomato Basil Soup

Ingredients:

- 4 lbs tomatoes, washed and chopped
- 2 onions, chopped
- 4 cloves garlic, minced
- 1/4 cup olive oil

- 4 cups vegetable broth
- 1/2 cup fresh basil leaves, chopped
- Salt and pepper to taste

Instructions:

1. In a large pot, heat olive oil over medium heat. Add onions and garlic, sauté until soft.
2. Add chopped tomatoes and vegetable broth to the pot. Bring to a boil, then reduce heat and simmer for 20-25 minutes.
3. Stir in fresh basil leaves, salt, and pepper. Cook for an additional 5 minutes.
4. Use an immersion blender to puree the soup until smooth.
5. Ladle hot soup into sterilized jars, leaving 1-inch headspace.
6. Wipe jar rims, apply lids, and tighten bands finger-tight.
7. Process jars in a pressure canner at 10 pounds pressure for 75 minutes for pint jars or 90 minutes for quart jars.
8. Allow jars to cool, then check seals and store in a cool, dark place.

Shelf Life: Up to 1 year.

24. Mango Salsa

Ingredients:

- 4 cups diced mango
- 2 cups diced red bell pepper

- 1 cup diced red onion
- 1/2 cup chopped fresh cilantro
- 1/4 cup lime juice
- 2 tbsp diced jalapeno peppers
- 1 tsp salt

Instructions:

1. In a large bowl, combine diced mango, red bell pepper, red onion, cilantro, lime juice, jalapeno peppers, and salt. Mix well.
2. Ladle salsa into sterilized jars, leaving 1/2-inch headspace.
3. Wipe jar rims, apply lids, and tighten bands finger-tight.
4. Process jars in a pressure canner at 5 pounds pressure for 10 minutes.
5. Allow jars to cool, then check seals and store in a cool, dark place.

Shelf Life: Up to 1 year.

25. Peach BBQ Sauce

Ingredients:

- 6 cups peeled, pitted, and chopped peaches
- 2 cups apple cider vinegar
- 1 cup brown sugar
- 1 cup ketchup
- 1/2 cup molasses

- 1/4 cup Worcestershire sauce

- 2 tbsp Dijon mustard

- 2 cloves garlic, minced

- 1 tsp smoked paprika

- 1 tsp salt

- 1/2 tsp black pepper

Instructions:

1. In a large pot, combine chopped peaches, apple cider vinegar, brown sugar, ketchup, molasses, Worcestershire sauce, Dijon mustard, garlic, paprika, salt, and black pepper.

2. Bring mixture to a boil over medium-high heat, then reduce heat and simmer for 45-60 minutes, stirring occasionally, until sauce thickens.

3. Ladle hot BBQ sauce into sterilized jars, leaving 1/2-inch headspace.

4. Wipe jar rims, apply lids, and tighten bands finger-tight.

5. Process jars in a pressure canner at 10 pounds pressure for 10 minutes.

6. Allow jars to cool, then check seals and store in a cool, dark place.

Shelf Life: Up to 1 year.

26. Mixed Berry Jam

Ingredients:

- 4 cups mixed berries (strawberries, blueberries, raspberries, blackberries)

- 2 cups granulated sugar
- 1/4 cup lemon juice
- 1 tsp vanilla extract (optional)

Instructions:

1. In a large pot, combine mixed berries, sugar, lemon juice, and vanilla extract. Let sit for 2 hours to allow the sugar to draw out the juices.
2. Bring berry mixture to a boil over medium-high heat, stirring frequently.
3. Continue boiling until jam reaches gel stage, about 20-30 minutes.
4. Ladle hot jam into sterilized jars, leaving 1/4-inch headspace.
5. Wipe jar rims, apply lids, and tighten bands finger-tight.
6. Process jars in a pressure canner at 5 pounds pressure for 5 minutes.
7. Allow jars to cool, then check seals and store in a cool, dark place.

Shelf Life: Up to 1 year.

27. Vegetable Stock

Ingredients:

- Assorted vegetable scraps (carrot peels, onion ends, celery leaves, etc.)
- 1 onion, chopped
- 2 carrots, chopped
- 2 celery stalks, chopped
- 4 cloves garlic, smashed

- 2 bay leaves
- 1 tbsp whole peppercorns
- Water

Instructions:

1. In a large pot, combine vegetable scraps, chopped onion, carrots, celery, garlic, bay leaves, and peppercorns.
2. Cover ingredients with water, ensuring they are fully submerged.
3. Bring mixture to a boil, then reduce heat and simmer for 1-2 hours, until stock is flavorful and vegetables are soft.
4. Strain stock through a fine-mesh sieve or cheesecloth to remove solids.
5. Ladle hot vegetable stock into sterilized jars, leaving 1-inch headspace.
6. Wipe jar rims, apply lids, and tighten bands finger-tight.
7. Process jars in a pressure canner at 10 pounds pressure for 25 minutes for pint jars or 30 minutes for quart jars.
8. Allow jars to cool, then check seals and store in a cool, dark place.

Shelf Life: Up to 1 year.

28. Pickled Beets

Ingredients:

- 4 lbs beets, washed, peeled, and sliced
- 2 cups white vinegar

- 2 cups water

- 1 cup granulated sugar

- 2 tsp pickling salt

- 1 tsp whole cloves

- 1 tsp whole allspice berries

- 1 cinnamon stick

Instructions:

1. In a saucepan, combine white vinegar, water, sugar, pickling salt, cloves, allspice berries, and cinnamon stick. Bring to a boil.
2. Pack sliced beets into sterilized jars, leaving 1/2-inch headspace.
3. Pour hot pickling liquid over beets, covering them completely and leaving 1/2-inch headspace.
4. Wipe jar rims, apply lids, and tighten bands finger-tight.
5. Process jars in a pressure canner at 10 pounds pressure for 30 minutes.
6. Allow jars to cool, then check seals and store in a cool, dark place.

Shelf Life: Up to 1 year.

29. Peach Salsa

Ingredients:

- 4 cups diced peaches

- 2 cups diced red bell pepper

- 1 cup diced red onion
- 1/2 cup chopped fresh cilantro
- 1/4 cup lime juice
- 2 tbsp diced jalapeno peppers
- 1 tsp salt

Instructions:

1. In a large bowl, combine diced peaches, red bell pepper, red onion, cilantro, lime juice, jalapeno peppers, and salt. Mix well.
2. Ladle salsa into sterilized jars, leaving 1/2-inch headspace.
3. Wipe jar rims, apply lids, and tighten bands finger-tight.
4. Process jars in a pressure canner at 5 pounds pressure for 10 minutes.
5. Allow jars to cool, then check seals and store in a cool, dark place.

Shelf Life: Up to 1 year.

30. Lemon Garlic Asparagus

Ingredients:

- 4 lbs asparagus, trimmed
- 4 cloves garlic, minced
- Zest of 2 lemons
- 1/4 cup lemon juice
- 2 cups water

- 2 tsp salt

Instructions:

1. In a large pot, bring water to a boil. Add salt and asparagus spears, blanch for 2-3 minutes.
2. Remove asparagus from boiling water and immediately plunge into ice water to stop cooking. Drain and set aside.
3. In a small saucepan, combine minced garlic, lemon zest, lemon juice, and water. Bring to a boil, then reduce heat and simmer for 5 minutes.
4. Pack blanched asparagus spears into sterilized jars, standing them upright.
5. Pour hot lemon garlic mixture over asparagus, covering them completely and leaving 1/2-inch headspace.
6. Wipe jar rims, apply lids, and tighten bands finger-tight.
7. Process jars in a pressure canner at 10 pounds pressure for 10 minutes.
8. Allow jars to cool, then check seals and store in a cool, dark place.

Shelf Life: Up to 1 year.

31. Mango Chutney

Ingredients:

- 6 cups diced mango
- 2 cups apple cider vinegar
- 2 cups granulated sugar

- 1 cup raisins
- 1 cup chopped onion
- 1/4 cup crystallized ginger, chopped
- 2 cloves garlic, minced
- 1 tbsp mustard seeds
- 1 tsp ground cinnamon
- 1/2 tsp ground cloves
- 1/2 tsp salt

Instructions:

1. In a large pot, combine diced mango, apple cider vinegar, sugar, raisins, onion, crystallized ginger, garlic, mustard seeds, cinnamon, cloves, and salt.
2. Bring mixture to a boil over medium-high heat, then reduce heat and simmer for 45-60 minutes, stirring occasionally, until chutney thickens.
3. Ladle hot chutney into sterilized jars, leaving 1/2-inch headspace.
4. Wipe jar rims, apply lids, and tighten bands finger-tight.
5. Process jars in a pressure canner at 10 pounds pressure for 10 minutes.
6. Allow jars to cool, then check seals and store in a cool, dark place.

Shelf Life: Up to 1 year.

32. Cinnamon Applesauce

Ingredients:

- 5 lbs apples, peeled, cored, and chopped
- 1 cup water
- 1/2 cup granulated sugar
- 1 tsp ground cinnamon
- 1/4 tsp ground nutmeg

Instructions:

1. In a large pot, combine chopped apples and water. Cook over medium heat until apples are soft, about 20-25 minutes.
2. Use a potato masher or immersion blender to mash apples to desired consistency.
3. Stir in sugar, cinnamon, and nutmeg.
4. Ladle hot applesauce into sterilized jars, leaving 1/2-inch headspace.
5. Wipe jar rims, apply lids, and tighten bands finger-tight.
6. Process jars in a pressure canner at 5 pounds pressure for 5 minutes.
7. Allow jars to cool, then check seals and store in a cool, dark place.

Shelf Life: Up to 1 year.

33. Tomato Jam

Ingredients:

- 4 lbs tomatoes, washed and chopped
- 2 cups granulated sugar

- 1/4 cup apple cider vinegar
- Zest and juice of 2 lemons
- 1 tsp ground ginger
- 1/2 tsp ground cinnamon
- 1/4 tsp ground cloves
- 1/4 tsp ground allspice
- 1/4 tsp salt

Instructions:

1. In a large pot, combine chopped tomatoes, sugar, apple cider vinegar, lemon zest, lemon juice, ginger, cinnamon, cloves, allspice, and salt.
2. Bring mixture to a boil over medium-high heat, stirring frequently.
3. Reduce heat and simmer for 1-1.5 hours, until jam thickens and reaches desired consistency.
4. Ladle hot jam into sterilized jars, leaving 1/4-inch headspace.
5. Wipe jar rims, apply lids, and tighten bands finger-tight.
6. Process jars in a pressure canner at 5 pounds pressure for 10 minutes.
7. Allow jars to cool, then check seals and store in a cool, dark place.

Shelf Life: Up to 1 year.

34. Pumpkin Butter

Ingredients:

- 4 cups pumpkin puree
- 2 cups apple cider
- 1 1/2 cups granulated sugar
- 1/4 cup lemon juice
- 2 tsp ground cinnamon
- 1/2 tsp ground ginger
- 1/4 tsp ground cloves
- 1/4 tsp ground nutmeg

Instructions:

1. In a large pot, combine pumpkin puree, apple cider, sugar, lemon juice, cinnamon, ginger, cloves, and nutmeg.
2. Bring mixture to a boil over medium-high heat, stirring frequently.
3. Reduce heat and simmer for 30-45 minutes, until pumpkin butter thickens and reaches desired consistency.
4. Ladle hot pumpkin butter into sterilized jars, leaving 1/4-inch headspace.
5. Wipe jar rims, apply lids, and tighten bands finger-tight.
6. Process jars in a pressure canner at 5 pounds pressure for 10 minutes.
7. Allow jars to cool, then check seals and store in a cool, dark place.

Shelf Life: Up to 1 year.

35. Ginger Pear Preserves

Ingredients:

- 4 cups diced pears
- 2 cups granulated sugar
- 1/4 cup lemon juice
- 2 tbsp fresh ginger, grated
- Zest of 1 lemon

Instructions:

1. In a large pot, combine diced pears, sugar, lemon juice, grated ginger, and lemon zest. Let sit for 2 hours to allow the sugar to draw out the juices.
2. Bring pear mixture to a boil over medium-high heat, stirring frequently.
3. Reduce heat and simmer for 30-40 minutes, until preserves thicken and reach desired consistency.
4. Ladle hot preserves into sterilized jars, leaving 1/4-inch headspace.
5. Wipe jar rims, apply lids, and tighten bands finger-tight.
6. Process jars in a pressure canner at 5 pounds pressure for 10 minutes.
7. Allow jars to cool, then check seals and store in a cool, dark place.

Shelf Life: Up to 1 year.

36. Spicy Pickled Okra

Ingredients:

- 4 lbs fresh okra
- 4 cloves garlic, peeled
- 4 small hot peppers
- 4 sprigs fresh dill
- 4 cups white vinegar
- 4 cups water
- 1/4 cup pickling salt
- 2 tbsp pickling spice

Instructions:

1. In each sterilized jar, place 1 garlic clove, 1 hot pepper, and 1 sprig of dill.
2. Pack okra tightly into jars, leaving 1/2-inch headspace.
3. In a saucepan, combine white vinegar, water, pickling salt, and pickling spice. Bring to a boil.
4. Pour hot brine over okra, covering them completely and leaving 1/2-inch headspace.
5. Wipe jar rims, apply lids, and tighten bands finger-tight.
6. Process jars in a pressure canner at 10 pounds pressure for 10 minutes.
7. Allow jars to cool, then check seals and store in a cool, dark place.

Shelf Life: Up to 1 year.

37. Honey Cinnamon Pear Butter

Ingredients:

- 5 lbs ripe pears, peeled, cored, and chopped
- 1/4 cup honey
- 1/4 cup lemon juice
- 2 tsp ground cinnamon
- 1/4 tsp ground nutmeg

Instructions:

1. In a large pot, combine chopped pears, honey, lemon juice, cinnamon, and nutmeg.
2. Cook pear mixture over medium heat, stirring frequently, until pears are soft and mixture thickens, about 30-40 minutes.
3. Use an immersion blender to puree the mixture until smooth.
4. Ladle hot pear butter into sterilized jars, leaving 1/4-inch headspace.
5. Wipe jar rims, apply lids, and tighten bands finger-tight.
6. Process jars in a pressure canner at 5 pounds pressure for 10 minutes.
7. Allow jars to cool, then check seals and store in a cool, dark place.

Shelf Life: Up to 1 year.

38. Peach Pie Filling

Ingredients:

- 8 cups peeled, pitted, and sliced peaches
- 2 cups granulated sugar
- 1/2 cup cornstarch
- 1/4 cup lemon juice
- 1 tsp ground cinnamon
- 1/4 tsp ground nutmeg

Instructions:

1. In a large pot, combine sliced peaches, sugar, cornstarch, lemon juice, cinnamon, and nutmeg. Cook over medium heat until mixture thickens, stirring constantly.
2. Remove from heat and let cool slightly.
3. Ladle hot pie filling into sterilized jars, leaving 1-inch headspace.
4. Wipe jar rims, apply lids, and tighten bands finger-tight.
5. Process jars in a pressure canner at 10 pounds pressure for 20 minutes.
6. Allow jars to cool, then check seals and store in a cool, dark place.

Shelf Life: Up to 1 year.

39. Chunky Tomato Sauce

Ingredients:

- 8 lbs tomatoes, washed and chopped
- 2 onions, chopped
- 4 cloves garlic, minced
- 1/4 cup olive oil
- 2 tsp dried basil
- 2 tsp dried oregano
- 2 tsp salt
- 1/2 tsp black pepper

Instructions:

1. In a large pot, heat olive oil over medium heat. Add onions and garlic, sauté until soft.
2. Add chopped tomatoes to the pot. Stir in basil, oregano, salt, and black pepper.
3. Cook tomato sauce over medium heat for 45-60 minutes, stirring occasionally, until sauce thickens.
4. Ladle hot sauce into sterilized jars, leaving 1-inch headspace.
5. Wipe jar rims, apply lids, and tighten bands finger-tight.
6. Process jars in a pressure canner at 10 pounds pressure for 40 minutes for pint jars or 45 minutes for quart jars.
7. Allow jars to cool, then check seals and store in a cool, dark place.

Shelf Life: Up to 1 year.

40. Orange Marmalade

Ingredients:

- 4 cups orange slices (about 4 large oranges)
- 2 cups water
- 4 cups granulated sugar
- Zest and juice of 1 lemon

Instructions:

1. In a large pot, combine orange slices, water, sugar, lemon zest, and lemon juice. Bring to a boil over medium-high heat, stirring frequently.
2. Reduce heat and simmer for 45-60 minutes, until marmalade thickens and reaches desired consistency.
3. Ladle hot marmalade into sterilized jars, leaving 1/4-inch headspace.
4. Wipe jar rims, apply lids, and tighten bands finger-tight.
5. Process jars in a pressure canner at 5 pounds pressure for 10 minutes.
6. Allow jars to cool, then check seals and store in a cool, dark place.

Shelf Life: Up to 1 year.

41. Black Bean and Corn Salsa

Ingredients:

- 4 cups black beans, cooked
- 2 cups corn kernels (fresh or frozen)
- 1 cup diced tomatoes
- 1/2 cup diced red onion
- 1/4 cup chopped fresh cilantro
- 1/4 cup lime juice
- 2 tbsp diced jalapeno peppers
- 1 tsp ground cumin
- 1/2 tsp salt

Instructions:

1. In a large bowl, combine black beans, corn kernels, diced tomatoes, red onion, cilantro, lime juice, jalapeno peppers, cumin, and salt. Mix well.
2. Ladle salsa into sterilized jars, leaving 1/2-inch headspace.
3. Wipe jar rims, apply lids, and tighten bands finger-tight.
4. Process jars in a pressure canner at 5 pounds pressure for 10 minutes.
5. Allow jars to cool, then check seals and store in a cool, dark place.

Shelf Life: Up to 1 year.

42. Strawberry Rhubarb Jam

Ingredients:

- 4 cups diced rhubarb
- 4 cups sliced strawberries
- 4 cups granulated sugar
- 1/4 cup lemon juice
- Zest of 1 lemon

Instructions:

1. In a large pot, combine diced rhubarb, sliced strawberries, sugar, lemon juice, and lemon zest. Let sit for 2 hours to allow the sugar to draw out the juices.
2. Bring fruit mixture to a boil over medium-high heat, stirring frequently.
3. Continue boiling until jam reaches gel stage, about 20-30 minutes.
4. Ladle hot jam into sterilized jars, leaving 1/4-inch headspace.
5. Wipe jar rims, apply lids, and tighten bands finger-tight.
6. Process jars in a pressure canner at 5 pounds pressure for 5 minutes.
7. Allow jars to cool, then check seals and store in a cool, dark place.

Shelf Life: Up to 1 year.

43. Roasted Red Pepper Sauce

Ingredients:

- 8 large red bell peppers
- 2 onions, chopped
- 4 cloves garlic, minced
- 1/4 cup olive oil
- 2 cups vegetable broth
- 2 tsp dried thyme
- 2 tsp dried basil
- 2 tsp salt
- 1 tsp black pepper

Instructions:

1. Preheat oven to 400°F (200°C). Place whole red bell peppers on a baking sheet and roast in the oven for 30-40 minutes, until skins are charred and blistered.
2. Remove peppers from the oven and transfer to a bowl. Cover the bowl with plastic wrap and let peppers steam for 10 minutes.
3. Peel off the skins of the roasted peppers, remove stems and seeds, and chop the flesh.
4. In a large pot, heat olive oil over medium heat. Add chopped onions and garlic, sauté until soft.
5. Add chopped roasted red peppers, vegetable broth, thyme, basil, salt, and black pepper to the pot. Bring to a boil, then reduce heat and simmer for 20-25 minutes.

6. Use an immersion blender to puree the sauce until smooth.

7. Ladle hot sauce into sterilized jars, leaving 1-inch headspace.

8. Wipe jar rims, apply lids, and tighten bands finger-tight.

9. Process jars in a pressure canner at 10 pounds pressure for 40 minutes for pint jars or 45 minutes for quart jars.

10. Allow jars to cool, then check seals and store in a cool, dark place.

Shelf Life: Up to 1 year.

44. Peach Chutney

Ingredients:

- 6 cups diced peaches
- 2 cups apple cider vinegar
- 2 cups brown sugar
- 1 cup raisins
- 1 cup chopped onion
- 1/4 cup crystallized ginger, chopped
- 2 cloves garlic, minced
- 1 tbsp mustard seeds
- 1 tsp ground cinnamon
- 1/2 tsp ground cloves
- 1/2 tsp salt

Instructions:

1. In a large pot, combine diced peaches, apple cider vinegar, brown sugar, raisins, onion, crystallized ginger, garlic, mustard seeds, cinnamon, cloves, and salt.

2. Bring mixture to a boil over medium-high heat, then reduce heat and simmer for 45-60 minutes, stirring occasionally, until chutney thickens.

3. Ladle hot chutney into sterilized jars, leaving 1/2-inch headspace.

4. Wipe jar rims, apply lids, and tighten bands finger-tight.

5. Process jars in a pressure canner at 10 pounds pressure for 10 minutes.

6. Allow jars to cool, then check seals and store in a cool, dark place.

Shelf Life: Up to 1 year.

45. Spiced Pear Butter

Ingredients:

- 5 lbs ripe pears, peeled, cored, and chopped
- 2 cups apple cider
- 1 1/2 cups granulated sugar
- 1/4 cup lemon juice
- 2 tsp ground cinnamon
- 1/2 tsp ground cloves
- 1/4 tsp ground nutmeg

Instructions:

1. In a large pot, combine chopped pears, apple cider, sugar, lemon juice, cinnamon, cloves, and nutmeg.
2. Cook pear mixture over medium heat, stirring frequently, until pears are soft and mixture thickens, about 30-40 minutes.
3. Use an immersion blender to puree the mixture until smooth.
4. Ladle hot pear butter into sterilized jars, leaving 1/4-inch headspace.
5. Wipe jar rims, apply lids, and tighten bands finger-tight.
6. Process jars in a pressure canner at 5 pounds pressure for 10 minutes.
7. Allow jars to cool, then check seals and store in a cool, dark place.

Shelf Life: Up to 1 year.

46. Cranberry Orange Relish

Ingredients:

- 4 cups fresh or frozen cranberries
- 2 oranges, peeled and chopped
- 2 cups granulated sugar
- 1/4 cup orange juice
- Zest of 1 orange

Instructions:

1. In a food processor, pulse cranberries until coarsely chopped.

2. Transfer chopped cranberries to a large pot. Add chopped oranges, sugar, orange juice, and orange zest.

3. Bring mixture to a boil over medium-high heat, stirring frequently.

4. Reduce heat and simmer for 20-25 minutes, until relish thickens.

5. Ladle hot relish into sterilized jars, leaving 1/4-inch headspace.

6. Wipe jar rims, apply lids, and tighten bands finger-tight.

7. Process jars in a pressure canner at 5 pounds pressure for 10 minutes.

8. Allow jars to cool, then check seals and store in a cool, dark place.

Shelf Life: Up to 1 year.

47. Mango Habanero Salsa

Ingredients:

- 4 cups diced mango
- 2 habanero peppers, seeded and finely chopped
- 1 cup diced red onion
- 1/4 cup chopped fresh cilantro
- 1/4 cup lime juice
- 1 tsp salt

Instructions:

1. In a large bowl, combine diced mango, chopped habanero peppers, red onion, cilantro, lime juice, and salt. Mix well.
2. Ladle salsa into sterilized jars, leaving 1/2-inch headspace.
3. Wipe jar rims, apply lids, and tighten bands finger-tight.
4. Process jars in a pressure canner at 5 pounds pressure for 10 minutes.
5. Allow jars to cool, then check seals and store in a cool, dark place.

Shelf Life: Up to 1 year.

48. Apple Pie Filling

Ingredients:

- 8 cups peeled, cored, and sliced apples
- 2 cups granulated sugar
- 1/2 cup cornstarch
- 1/4 cup lemon juice
- 1 tsp ground cinnamon
- 1/4 tsp ground nutmeg

Instructions:

1. In a large pot, combine sliced apples, sugar, cornstarch, lemon juice, cinnamon, and nutmeg. Cook over medium heat until mixture thickens, stirring constantly.
2. Remove from heat and let cool slightly.

3. Ladle hot pie filling into sterilized jars, leaving 1-inch headspace.

4. Wipe jar rims, apply lids, and tighten bands finger-tight.

5. Process jars in a pressure canner at 10 pounds pressure for 20 minutes.

6. Allow jars to cool, then check seals and store in a cool, dark place.

Shelf Life: Up to 1 year.

49. Spicy Tomato Jam

Ingredients:

- 4 lbs tomatoes, washed and chopped
- 2 cups granulated sugar
- 1/4 cup apple cider vinegar
- Zest and juice of 2 limes
- 2 jalapeno peppers, seeded and finely chopped
- 2 cloves garlic, minced
- 1 tsp ground cumin
- 1/2 tsp ground coriander
- 1/4 tsp cayenne pepper
- 1/4 tsp salt

Instructions:

1. In a large pot, combine chopped tomatoes, sugar, apple cider vinegar, lime zest, lime juice, jalapeno peppers, garlic, cumin, coriander, cayenne pepper, and salt.

2. Bring mixture to a boil over medium-high heat, stirring frequently.

3. Reduce heat and simmer for 1-1.5 hours, until jam thickens and reaches desired consistency.

4. Ladle hot jam into sterilized jars, leaving 1/4-inch headspace.

5. Wipe jar rims, apply lids, and tighten bands finger-tight.

6. Process jars in a pressure canner at 5 pounds pressure for 10 minutes.

7. Allow jars to cool, then check seals and store in a cool, dark place.

Shelf Life: Up to 1 year.

50. Pineapple Jalapeno Jelly

Ingredients:

- 4 cups diced pineapple
- 2 cups apple cider vinegar
- 2 cups granulated sugar
- 2 jalapeno peppers, seeded and finely chopped
- 1/4 cup lemon juice
- 1 packet powdered pectin

Instructions:

1. In a blender or food processor, puree diced pineapple until smooth.

2. In a large pot, combine pureed pineapple, apple cider vinegar, sugar, chopped jalapeno peppers, and lemon juice.

3. Bring mixture to a boil over medium-high heat, stirring frequently.

4. Once boiling, add powdered pectin and continue to boil for 1 minute, stirring constantly.

5. Remove from heat and skim off any foam.

6. Ladle hot jelly into sterilized jars, leaving 1/4-inch headspace.

7. Wipe jar rims, apply lids, and tighten bands finger-tight.

8. Process jars in a pressure canner at 5 pounds pressure for 10 minutes.

9. Allow jars to cool, then check seals and store in a cool, dark place.

Shelf Life: Up to 1 year.

Made in United States
Troutdale, OR
04/23/2024

19382939R00040